SYSTEMS IN THE SPECIAL EDUCATION CLASSROOM

Create and use systems for your classroom to increase organization, efficiency, and time!

SABRINA CREWS

Ms. Crews' Classroom Creations

Published by Ms. Crews' Classroom Creations, LLC
Nashville, Tn
www.mscrewsclassroomcreations.com

© 2020 Sabrina Crews
Photographs © Sabrina Crews

Printed in the United States of America

ISBN 978 1 7363333 1 0 (paperback)
ISBN 978 1 736333 0 3 (ebook)

TABLE OF CONTENTS

Introduction

What are systems?

Before we can dive into using systems in our classrooms, we need to agree on a definition. Systems provide the basic steps of how you complete a specific task. Think of systems as a task analysis for adults.

I always like to think of this example given to me in college. Our professor had all the ingredients needed to make a peanut butter and jelly sandwich. We had to break down the steps and the professor could only do what we told her to do. If we said, take out bread, the professor would rip the bag open because we didn't tell her how to take out the bread. We needed to break it down to the basic steps; untwist the tie, open the bag and take out two slices of bread.

Untwist the twist tie	→	Open the bag	→	Take out 2 slices of bread

Think as if you were going to be doing a task analysis for a student. If you were to break apart the steps of the student going to the bathroom, you would include the steps of pulling down your pants, pulling down your underwear, sitting on the toilet, voiding in the toilet and so on. You get very specific with your steps.

This is exactly what systems are. They are a task analysis for adults. Systems break down the things that adults do into very detailed steps.

Why should you use systems?
Systems provide accountability and consistency.

Throughout the day there are many adults that come in and out of my classroom. These adults could be administrators, paraprofessionals, related service providers, substitutes, and parent volunteers. When you put systems in place, every adult, no matter how long or often they are in your room, knows exactly what they need to be doing. They also know what students they should work with and what they should work on curriculum wise.

Systems save time and are efficient. Think about that amount of time you spend explaining the daily routine or the daily expectations to the various adults in your room. When you systemize your classroom, you can spend your time on teaching the students instead of prepping the adults.

Systems also transfer easily from year to year. When you first set up systems in your classroom, you will spend some time prepping and outlining each system. Once outlined and set up, systems are relatively easy to manage. Systems give you back some of your time to use daily.

How can you use systems?

The first thing I recommend is starting with the most simplistic system: checklists. This could be as simple as a checklist for items paraprofessionals need to complete first thing in the morning. Then, I recommend you systemize everything. And yes, I mean everything. This may seem like a daunting task, but this book will help you work through the creation and implementation of your systems. Take it in bite-sized chunks and as you add more and more systems you will end up saving time and increasing your efficiency.

System Story

Before we dive into our first system, I want to share a story about a system I use in my classroom.

The beginning of the day or the beginning of the time a student is in my room is extremely important. How students enter the room sets up the student, their peers, and the tone for their time in my classroom. I created and implemented an entry system that ensures the students start their day with success.

I give each student a color and they know their color. When they walk into the classroom, immediately to their right, is a color-coded bin. Each bin is on a shelf. The shelf has space for any backpacks, coats, and lunchboxes they may have brought with them. When they come in, they know to put their items away and collect their color-coded bin. In each bin are all the items they may need for the day. This could include a visual schedule, morning work, communication methods, pencils, etc. Once they have their bin, they head to their assigned seat to work.

This system allows for the students to be independent and successful right from the start. They can complete this task without me being in the room. I spend the first month, at least, teaching this procedure to my students. I also use the first month to train my paraprofessionals on their part of this system.

While my students work through this system independently, my paraprofessionals are there to implement any individual behavior plans. The paraprofessionals also support the students to complete their morning work using the prompt hierarchy. I can focus on taking attendance, checking parent communication notebooks, and return any paperwork to the student folders thus, saving me time during my planning period.

Systems provide you with accountability, consistency, and efficiency. By the end of this book, you will have transformed your classroom into a systemized, organized, student-centered classroom.

SECTION 1: SYSTEMS FOR THE CLASSROOM

The first section of systems are those that will help you with setting up your classroom.

ENTRY SYSTEM

The first system we will focus on is your entry system. If you think back to the story I shared in the introduction, this was the first system that really made a difference in how I run my classroom.

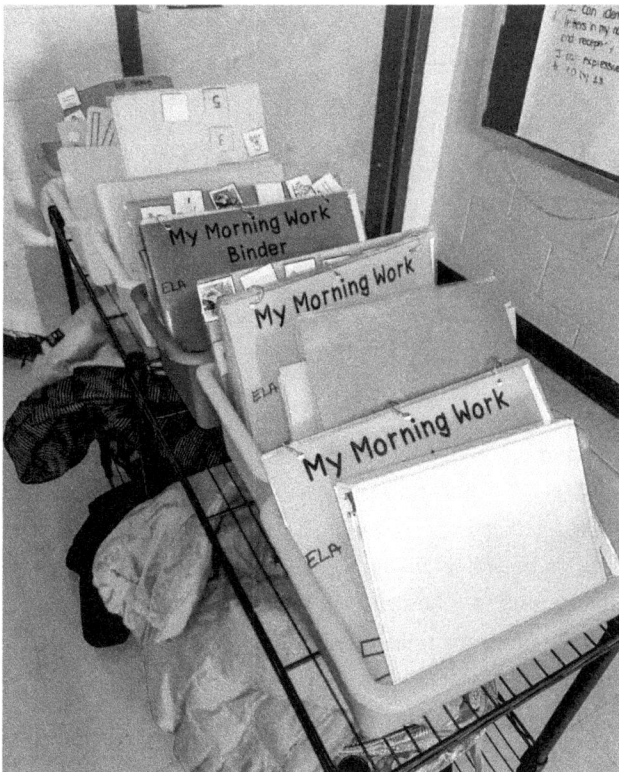

When you are planning your systems, you always want to start with clearly defined goals. What exactly do you want this system to accomplish? For the entry system, a possible goal could be to create an efficient, independent method for students to enter the classroom. You want to keep this goal in mind when you are planning and outlining your system. You also want to put the goal at the top of your system sheet.

Each system you create will have a system sheet. (see the appendix for example system sheets) This is the document outlines your system step by step. You can post this document in your classroom and store it in your lesson planning binder and sub binder.

Once you have set your entry system goal, the next question you want to ask is what the students will be doing. It is important to walk through all the steps to make sure you have outlined everything each student needs to do. Remember: systems are basically a task analysis.

In the entry system, your students might put away their backpacks and coats in their color-coded spot. They may need to put a folder or parent communication system in a set place, like a bucket. They may have materials they need to access, for example, a color-coded bin. And they may need to go to an assigned seat to work. Once you have listed everything you want your students to accomplish, go back and run through all of the steps again to make sure you have not missed anything.

After you have outlined everything the students will do, you will do the same thing for your paraprofessionals. What exactly do you need your paraprofessionals to be doing? For your entry system they may implement behavior plans and use token boards. They may also supervise students as they work through entering the classroom. The paraprofessionals may help students complete their morning work using the prompt hierarchy.

Last, you need to outline what you will do during the entry system. This could include things like checking folders for notes from home or responding to parent communication notebooks. You may need to take and submit attendance. You may also need to return paperwork to student folders to send home.

Once you have outlined exactly what each person will do during the system, you need to move on to determining what materials are needed to run this system. Think about the materials the students will need. For your entry system this could include a visual schedule, a communication binder, morning work, and a color-coded bin to hold these items.

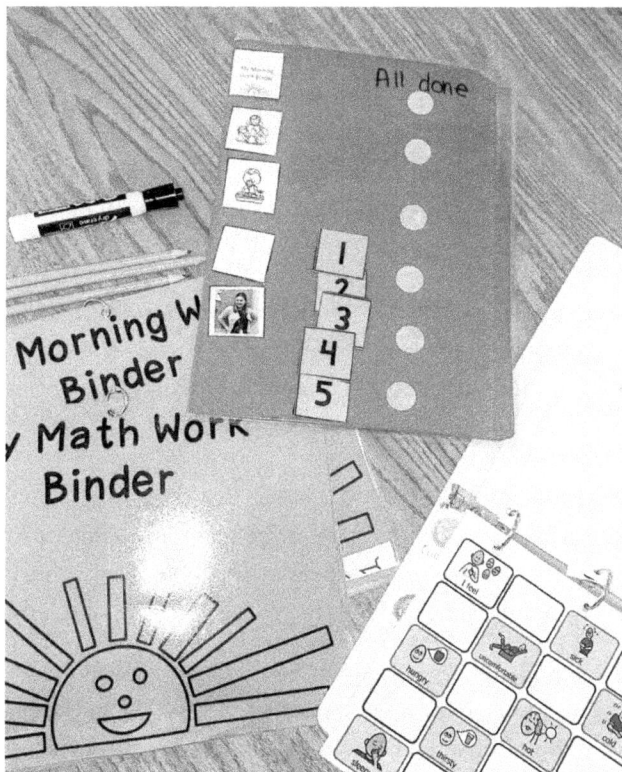

You also want to think about what materials the paraprofessionals may need. They might have a clipboard that holds the prompt hierarchy, copies of student behavior plans, and data sheets if you plan to take any data.

Now you may think that you are done with creating your system, but there are two more things you need to consider.

First, who will reset the system and how will they do it? The entry system is one that is relatively easy to reset. This usually includes resetting visual schedules for the next day, taking data on completed independent work and archiving any student work samples, erasing any dry erase morning work, and adding in any worksheets for the next day. I have my paraprofessionals reset the entry system before they leave for the day.

Second, you need to plan how you will teach this system to the students and the paraprofessionals. This involves directly teaching the system and using a video social story. It may include putting up visuals that show each step they need to complete. I recommend using pictures of your current students and videoing your current students working through the system.

When it comes to training my paraprofessionals, I like to teach them prior to the first day of school so they can help teach the students. We will go into more details about a system for training paraprofessionals in a later section of this book.

MATERIALS ORGANIZATION – MONTHLY BINS
Teachers are hoarders. Old curriculum you might use again, toilet paper rolls for a craft or a work task, the puzzle with the missing piece because it may show up next time you clean, etc.

Before I had a system to organize all my materials, I kept EVERYTHING, and I had no idea what I had. Sometimes I would even go buy more paint just to find that exact color in my cabinet two weeks later.

Now, with my systems in place, I know everything I have in my room and I know where everything is. Everything has a place and there is a place for everything.

The first organizational system I recommend is monthly bins. This system is a great option for anyone who uses monthly themes in their classroom.

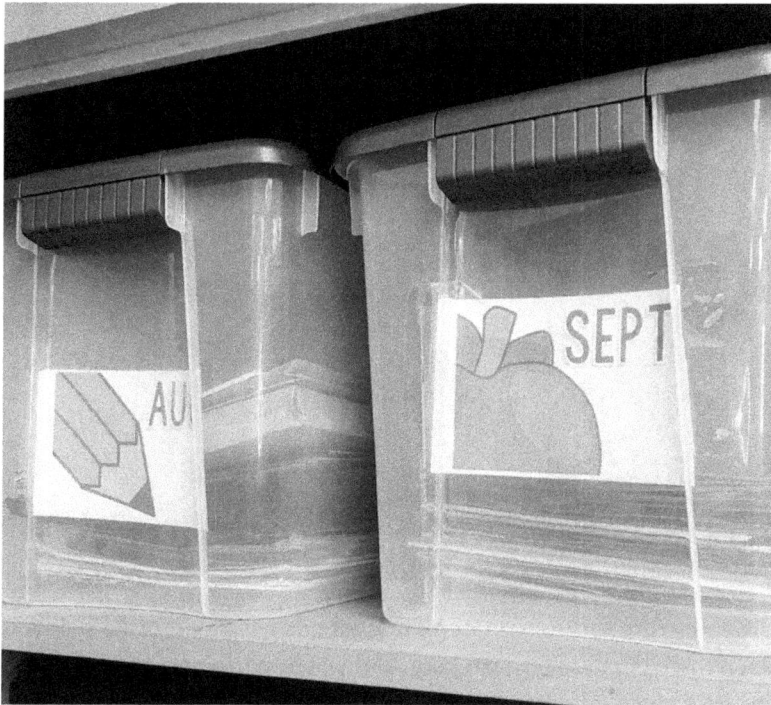

The first step in setting up your monthly bin system is to set your goal. For a monthly bin system, the goal could be to create an efficient way to manage materials that are needed in a specific month.

After you have set your goal, you need to determine the different categories of materials you will keep in your bin. For me this includes whole group materials, task cards, file folders, work tasks, sensory materials, and other related materials.

Once you have determined your categories, the next step is to sort out your items. This step is going to take the longest and require the most space. I recommend carving out a day and a space.

When I first made my monthly bins, I had set up a space for every month I would need. Our school year is August to May, so I had one section for each of the 10 months. I also set up a space for any materials I came across that did not belong in the monthly bins so I could sort those later.

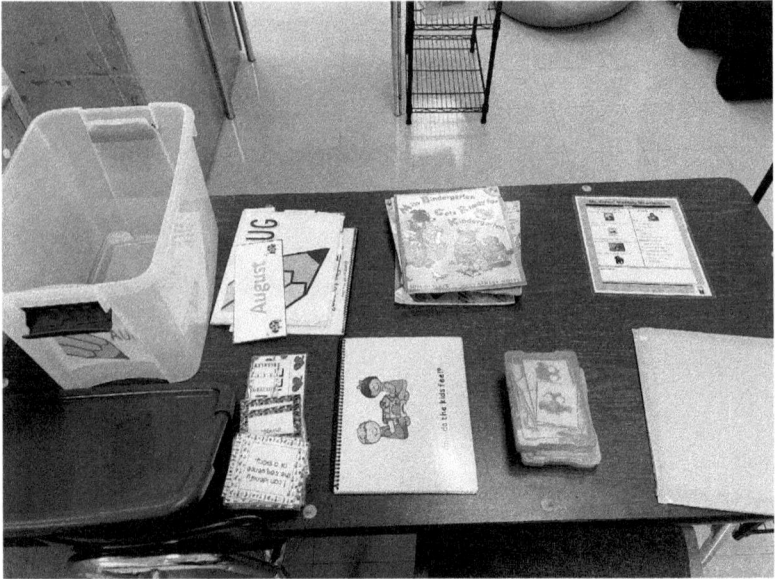

When you are sorting your items into monthly sections, make sure you keep them organized by category. This will be extremely helpful for the next step.

After you have placed everything in the correct monthly section, you need to create your inventory. This is where the magic of the system comes into play. The inventory sheet tells you exactly what is in your monthly bin. I keep my inventory sheet in the bin as well and in my teacher binder.

October

Books		Task Cards	
There Was An Old Lady Who Was Not Afraid of Anything		4 -There Was An Old Lady Who Was Not Afraid of Anything **errorless**	
Story boards, file folders, story cards – Not Afraid		1 -There Was An Old Lady Who Was Not Afraid of Anything **matching**	
The Three Bears			
Story boards, file folders, story cards – Three Bears		4 - The Three Bears **errorless**	
I Feel Silly		1 – The Three Bears **matching**	
Emotion cards		Emotions	
Question of the day book		2 – Counting **Halloween**	
10 fiction books		1 – Letter clip cards A-F	
5 fiction books		1 - Colors	
vocab cards		1 - Shapes	

File Folders	
2- Fall Patterns	
2 - Halloween Patterns	
Candy Color sort	
3 – Letter sorts , E, F, E/F	
1 – Letter sort A-D	

Play Materials	
I Spy Bottle	
10 PECs toy cards	
10 play scripts	

Other	
Fall Fest Letter	
Fall Fest Materials	
Fabric leaves for sensory table	
Sensory table toys	
Calendar pieces	
USB Drive with videos and smart board file	
Newsletter	
Lesson Plans	

I suggest breaking your inventory sheet into the categories you decided on above. My inventory sheets have whole group materials, task cards, file folders, work tasks, sensory materials, and other.

The last few steps to set up is to put monthly items into the correct labeled bin with the inventory sheet and then place a copy of your inventory sheet in your teaching binder. Finally, you will put your monthly bins away in the correct order.

Now each month you can grab the correct bin and have all the materials you need in one place. When you put everything away at the end of the month, use the inventory sheet to see what may have misplaced or ruined. Then you can add those items to your to do list to replace.

Even though I won't need the items for another year, I replace them as soon as possible. I don't want to get to next year and find that I am missing something. You will need to decide how and when you will handle replacements and add it to your system sheet. If you do not replace the items, make sure you update your inventory sheet.

MATERIALS ORGANIZATION – OTHER MATERIALS

Now that you have organized your monthly materials, you will need to plan out your system for organizing the rest of your items. I store my items in cabinets built into my classroom.

Just like all other systems, the first step it to set your goal. This could be to create an efficient way to organize and access materials used throughout the year.

Next, just like with the monthly bins, you want to categorize your materials. My categories are work tasks, art supplies, teaching materials, office back stock, sensory, functional play, cleaning supplies, and other.

You want to sort EVEYTHING into these categories. If something doesn't fit and you end up having a lot of that type of material, make a new category.

Once you have everything sorted, make your inventory sheets for each category. You will place this inventory sheet in your teacher binder and inside the cabinet where you will store the items.

The last step is to put all items in your cabinets using bins and dividers to organize everything. Ideally, you would have one cabinet for each category, but I know that is rarely an option.

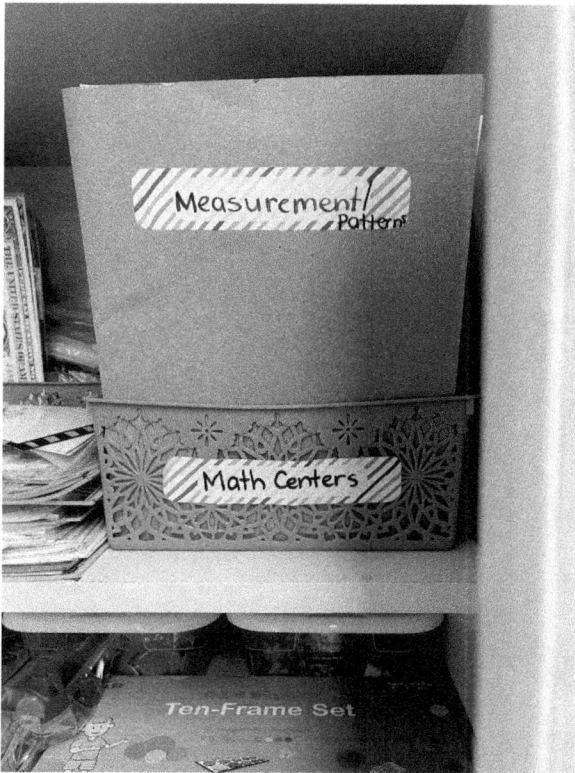

You need to label every cabinet so that anyone can easily find what they need without having to interrupt your teaching.

When you are looking for bins to place in your cabinets, I suggest the Dollar Tree or Target. You can also use empty cardboard boxes. It doesn't have to be fancy!

Since everything is already out, you will quickly be able to see what size and how many containers you will need. You also want to label your bins. For example, if your category is art supplies, you may have bins for crayons, markers, paint, etc.

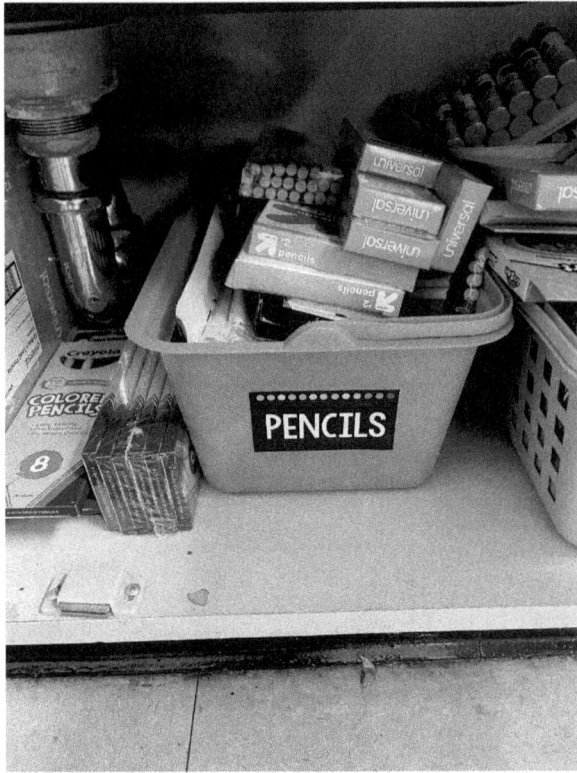

Throughout the year, as you are using and adding materials, make sure you update your inventory sheet. At the end of the year, I recommend replenishing anything you will need for next year and then updating and reprinting your inventory sheets. This will make the beginning of the year run smoother and allow you to spend less time prepping.

Visual Schedule System

The last system for classroom setup is your visual schedule system.

Again, you want to begin with setting your goal. For example, create and implement a visual schedule system that fosters independence in my students.

Even if you don't use individual visual schedules, try to have a class visual schedule. No matter who comes into your room, the visual schedule allows everyone to know what is going on in your classroom when.

I suggest using the same symbols or pictures for the class visual schedule and the students' individual schedules. The class visual schedule can simply live on a bulletin board or on a corkboard strip. However, you want to keep it as close to student eye level as possible.

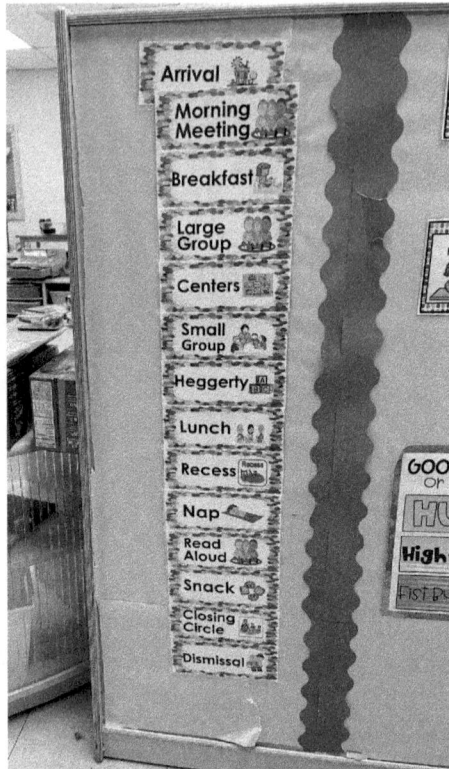

When you are thinking about setting up your student visual schedules, you first want to determine if you want the schedules to be fixed or mobile. Personally, I want my schedules to be mobile so when the students leave my room, they can take them with them and use the schedules in the general education classroom.

You need to determine how many schedule items each student can handle. Some of my students only have the next two items, some have five, and some have their entire day.

When you set up a fixed system, you want to have all visuals at the students' eye level. Each student will need their own "all done" place for their finished schedule pieces.

For mobile systems you have a few options. The one I use the most is a file folder. The front of the file folder has the upcoming schedule, and the inside holds the extra pieces.

You can use a pencil box or a photo case. This option is great for those students who may only have two or three schedule pieces at one time. The extra pieces and "all done" area can be the inside of the case.

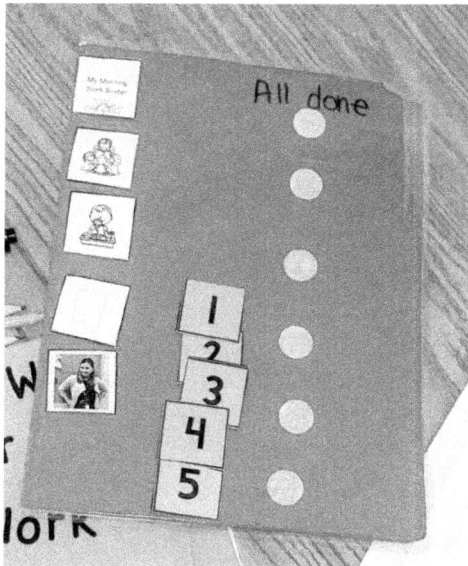

The last part of the system that you need to plan is how you will reset the schedules at the end of the day. I like to have my paraprofessionals use the instructional matrix (see section 4) to reset all the schedules as they rest the entry system.

SECTION 2: SYSTEMS FOR STUDENT BEHAVIOR

Student behavior can change the entire tone of the classroom. When you think about student behavior, there are three major aspects: proactive, individual, and reactive.

For all behavior systems, you need to be prepared for the unexpected. Having a large toolbox of strategies will support this.

It is important to note that with individual behavior systems and reactive behavior systems; it is likely the challenging behaviors will become more extreme before they improve. This is because they are trying to get the same reinforcement from their behavior that you are now withholding for the appropriate behavior.

For example, if a student is screaming to get out of completing an assignment and you introduce break cards, the screaming may get louder and louder as you wait for them to use a break card. If you stick with the interventions and stay consistent, the challenging behaviors will decrease, and the appropriate behavior will increase.

PROACTIVE BEHAVIOR SYSTEM

The proactive behavior system is your classroom management plan. The goal is to prevent any behaviors that may negatively impact the learning of the students in your classroom.

For this system you want to expect any potential setting events and antecedents and have an intervention in place to prevent them. You want to train any adults who will be in your classroom in each of the preventative interventions in your classroom. I also recommend making video social stories of each of the interventions using your current students. You can play these as the students need reminders.

The following is a list of preventative interventions you can implement in your classroom:

Behavior Momentum. Behavior momentum is an intervention where the students complete a series of quick and easy compliance tasks, to build up success and motivation, prior to a more challenging task.

Peace Corner. A peace corner is a section in your classroom where students can go when they need a break from a potentially "triggering" situation. The peace corner should include a timer students can set with a preset time limit. It needs to include de-escalation strategies the students can use to help with self-regulation, such as Zones of Regulation©.

Class Behavior Contract. As a class, you can come up with expectations for behavior and all students and teachers sign the contract.

Structure Work Systems. When you use structured work systems, you provide clear visual expectations and instructions for completing a task. Students have a set schedule of tasks to complete with the visual instructions. An example of this is the TEACHH© method for work systems.

Video Social Stories. Video social stories are a model of the skill or appropriate behavior used for teaching and reinforcing the skill or behavior.

Transition Supports. Transition supports include visual timers, visuals, predicable transitions, and signals for upcoming transitions.

Visual Schedules. Previously, we discussed a visual schedule system back in Section 1. The visual schedule provides visual structure to aid with transitions and increases predictability.

Use Predictable Routines. Having a consistent schedule will increase predictability and limit the interrupting questions of, "when is lunch".

Build in Breaks. When making your daily schedule, it is helpful to build in movement or brain breaks.

Give Praise. As much as possible, try to praise for appropriate behavior.

Build Relationships. All behavior is communication. If you can build a strong relationship with your class, you increase the likelihood of students communicating their needs in appropriate ways.

Individual Behavior Plan System

When it comes to individual behavior systems, the most important thing is to follow any Behavior Intervention Plans as written. You can definitely add interventions, but you need to follow those plans to stay in compliance.

Whether or not a student has an official behavior plan, you can set up behavior interventions to support those students who need it. The system I am going to walk you through creating is behavior bags.

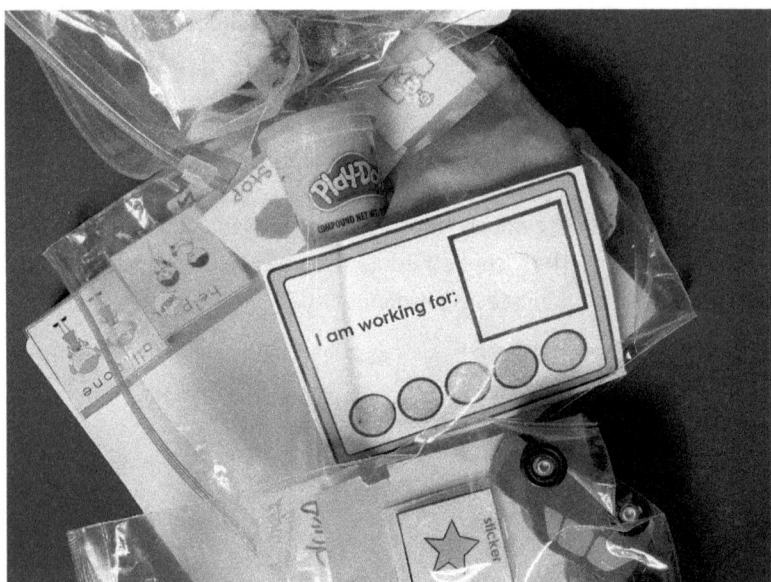

An example goal for the behavior bag system is to increase student independent with behavior regulation thus allowing them to participate in the classroom activities.

The first thing you need to determine is when the student will use the behavior bag. This will depend on the severity of the behavior and where it occurs. Some students may only use the bag in one class, while others may use the bag all day and take it with them from class to class.

The next question you need to answer is how they will get access to the bag. For some students, they can take it with them from class to class. Other students may need to have a bag in each classroom in a designated area they can access. And some students may need the teacher to give them their bag at the beginning of each class.

Once you have identified the when and how, you will then need to decide what will go in the bags. Each bag will be different as the student's needs will be the deciding factor. Some ideas of what to include are token boards, first then boards, calm down strategy cards, reward options (coloring pages, small toys, edibles), visual schedule, break cards, a copy of a behavior contract.

The last thing you will need to do is explicitly teach the behavior bag system to anyone involved. This includes any adult who will interact with the student. I recommend taking a video social story with the student using the items in the bag in the correct manner. This video can then be saved and viewed whenever the student may need a refresher. You can also use this to train any new adults who will work with the student.

The reactive behavior system you create will be a toolbox of strategies. You will need to determine which strategy is the best to use based on the behavior the student exhibits. The toolbox needs to be written down and shared with all the adults in the room. I recommend directly training the adults on each of the strategies you plan on using in your classroom. It is helpful to order the strategies in order from the least restrictive to the most restrictive. The following is a list of strategies and their definition:

Ignoring. For ignoring, you simply ignore the behavior. This includes all non-verbal communication.

Error Correction. For error correction, prompt (using the prompt hierarchy) the student to complete the behavior the correct way.

Response Interruption and Redirection. This strategy stops the inappropriate behavior by redirecting the student to a replacement behavior.

Positive Practice. When using positive practice, you will repetitively practice the appropriate behavior, giving positive praise each time.

Trauma-Informed De-Escalation. With de-escalation, the purpose is to de-escalate the challenging behavior. This can include leaving the student to experience their outburst and then reflecting when they have calmed down. Once the student is de-escalated, you can use another strategy to correct the behavior.

The next set of strategies are considered restrictive interventions and should be a last resort. You want to check with your district regarding policies for using restrictive interventions. If you need to use any of these and the student does not have a behavior plan in place, start the process of a behavior plan for the student.

Response Cost. Response cost refers to removing the reinforcement of an undesirable behavior. Please check with your district regarding policies for restrictive interventions prior to use.

Restitution. Restitution is used after the challenging behavior where the student restores the environment to how it existed prior to the behavior. Please check with your district regarding policies for restrictive interventions prior to use.

Non-Exclusionary Time Out. With non-exclusionary time you, you remove the student's ability to get a reinforcer without removing them from the setting. Please check with your district regarding policies for restrictive interventions prior to use.

Exclusionary Time Out. Exclusionary time out is when you remove the student from a reinforcing setting into a setting with a lower reinforcing value. Please check with your district regarding policies for restrictive interventions prior to use.

Section 3: Systems for Independent Work

When talking about independent work, I think of two different categories: seat work and work systems.

Seat Work System

You will set your seat work system up to cover any time the students are in their seats working independently, such as morning work or independent practice.

As with all systems, you want to start with your goal. A seat work system goal could be to implement a system for seat work that allows students to work independently with little to no assistance from adults.

The first thing you want to think about is when students will complete seat work. You want to make sure you have it clearly stated in your instructional matrix (see section 4). If you want them to do seat work more than once through the school day, you want to make sure your seat work system will work for all of those times.

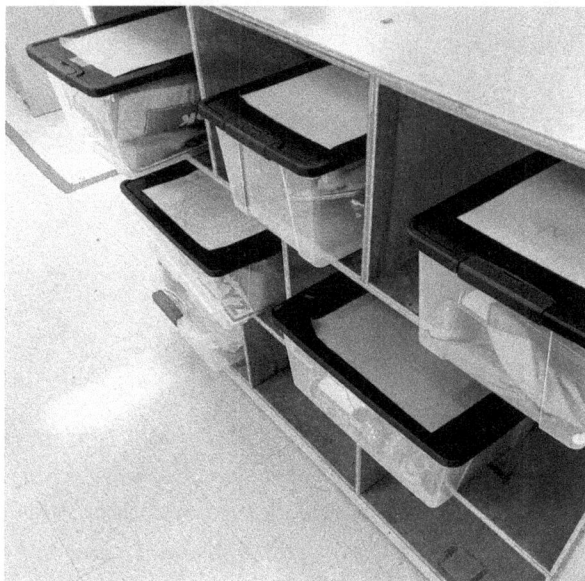

I recommend using a bin system for seat work. This will work for any time students need to work independently. The best thing about using a bin system is that you can add whatever you need for the day in the bin. I recommend numbering or color-coding the bins.

If you have any guides or handouts that students may need to access, such as a hundred chart and a word list, I recommend putting these in the bins and always keeping them in there for the students.

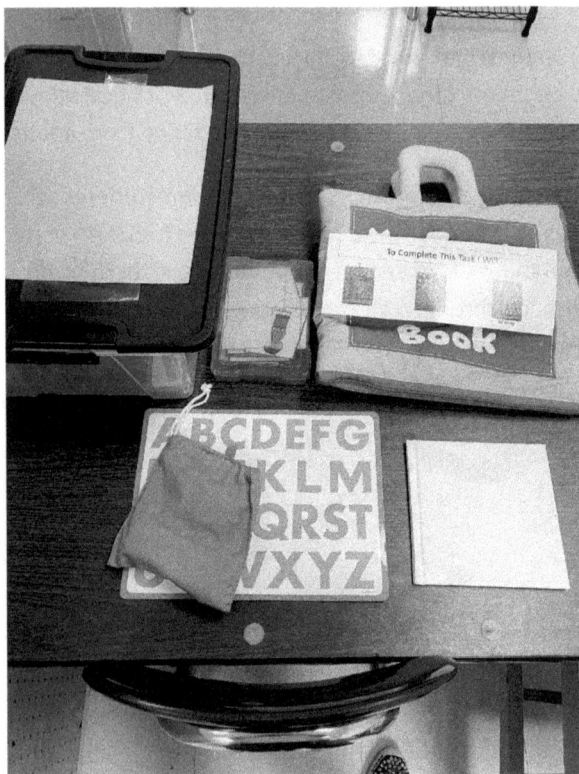

The next thing you will need to decide is when you will fill the bins with the independent seat work. A lot of this will depend on when you are using this system. I use my seat work system in the morning and for centers, so it is then refilled at the end of the day for the next morning.

If you use your seat work system multiple times a day, and do not want everything in there at once, you will need to have a set time you replace the work. You will also need to determine who is going to be filling the bins. I have my paraprofessionals erase any dry erase work and fill the bins with the work for the next day.

The work is already color coded, so they just have to match the worksheets with the correct bin. I make the copies on the colored paper during my planning period and label it with the day it is for. I like to make copies at least a week in advance, if not two weeks. You will need to decide how far ahead you want to make your copies.

Once copies are made, you need to determine how you will store the seat work. I like to put mine in file folders labeled with the day. The file folders are then put in a bin where the paraprofessionals can access it every afternoon.

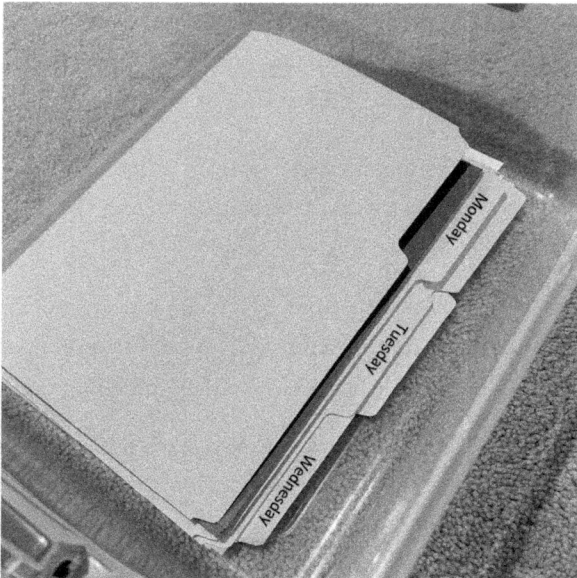

The last thing you need to think about is how you will handle answering questions during this time. There are a few ways you can handle this. One way is an "ask 3 before me", where the students have to ask 3 of their peers for help before asking you. This may not be possible in some of our classrooms. If that is the case, you can have a paraprofessional there to help the students with questions that may arise.

If you do not have a paraprofessional who can be around to facilitate, then you will want to have a signal for the students to know when they can come and ask you questions. This could be a special hat you wear or a touch light on your desk that when on, they can come and ask you, but when they need to continue to stay in their seat.

After you have determined when you will use the system, how you will store the work, who will fill/reset the system, and what you will do for questions, you need to train everyone who will be involved.

Again, I recommend directly training the adults and students. It is also a good idea to take a video of the students working through the system to save as a visual social story. You want to make sure you teach the students how to use any guides or materials you place in there also so they do not need to ask you for help.

STRUCTURED WORK SYSTEM

The next independent work system to plan is your structured work system. Work systems are a staple in self-contained special education classrooms. I recommend looking into the TEACCH® program if you haven't done so.

A goal for a structured work system could be to increase engagement, independence, and self-efficacy with task completion.

When planning your work system, you first want to think about where you will put it in your classroom. It is important that the students work from left to right. When they grab their first task, it will be on their left, and their "all done" area will be on the right. This means you need an area large enough to have space on either side of the student.

It is a helpful to plan to have the student space as free from distractions as possible. This could mean you put up desk dividers so they can focus on their work.

You then need to think what visuals you will need. You want to make a visual schedule for the order in which they should complete their tasks. You can use numbers, shapes, or even the picture of the task itself. You will want to have the label on the task and on the visual schedule. This allows the students to match the pictures to make sure they are completing the correct task.

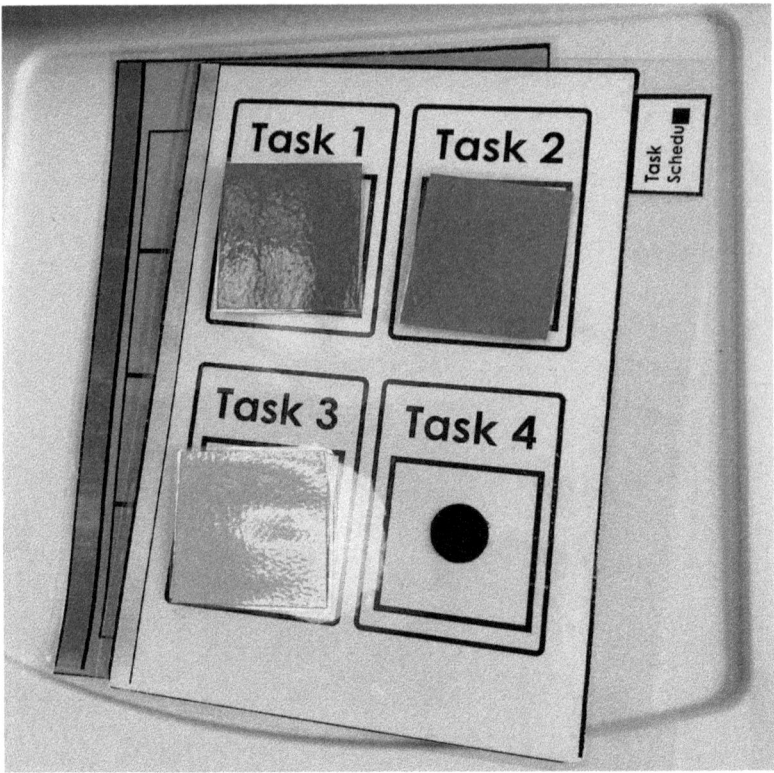

Then you want to think about any data you will collect, how you will collect it, and who will be collecting it. Data can be collected when you reset the work system. I recommend creating a data sheet you can have your paraprofessionals fill out as they reset the tasks and put them back in the starting area for each student.

The other thing you want to have is a sheet that includes all the tasks a specific student can complete or a schedule of which tasks each student should do each day. This way the paraprofessionals can complete the reset without asking you for help.

And finally, you want to make sure you are training everyone involved with this system. Again, I recommend taking a video social story for the students to review as they need reminders and directly training the adults.

Section 4: Systems for Working with Adults

Instructional Matrix

The first system to create for working with adults is the instructional matrix. An instructional matrix is a plan for what every single person, students and adults, is going to be doing within your classroom throughout the entire day. It is also called an activity matrix or zone planning.

An instructional matrix saves time by eliminating the need to tell everyone what they are doing throughout the day.

The goal for an instructional matrix is to outline your ideal day for every person who will be in your classroom.

You can make the instructional matrix in a table or using index cards and a bulletin board. The first step is to determine what timeframe you are going to use. I advise keeping it 30 minutes or less. I like to keep my timeframe as 15 minutes as most of my activities happen within 15 minutes.

Once you have determined your time frames, you want to start at the beginning of the day and place your times in the first column of your table.

Next, you will type in the activity you will complete during those timeframes. The overarching activity does not have to be lesson specific. For example, if you are working on phonics you will just write phonics, not a specific phonics skill.

You also want to split up any centers. So, if you have four literacy centers, you will write literacy center 1, literacy center 2, etc.

	A	B	C	D	E	F
1	TIME	Activity	Student(s)	Ms. Crews	Para 1	1-on-1
2	7:45	Arrival				
3	8:00	Inclusion				
4	8:15	Morning Work				
5	8:30	Morning Meeting				
6	8:45	Phonics				
7	9:00	Read Aloud				
8	9:15	ELA Center 1				
9	9:30	ELA Center 2				
10	9:45	ELA Center 3				
11	10:00	ELA Center 4				

The next step is to type in the names of the students who are in your classroom during each time frame. I recommend putting in the students' first names. This allows for a substitute to know exactly who should be in your room and when.

Once you have finished the first three columns, you then need to type in the names of all adults who are in room for 15 minutes or more in the first row starting at column four. Even if they are only in your room for 15 minutes, you still want to put them on your matrix.

If you choose, you can black out the times the person is not in your classroom.

	A	B	C	D	E	F
1	TIME	Activity	Student(s)	Ms. Crews	Para 1 - Lauren	1-on-1 - Ashley
2	7:45	Arrival	AN			
3	8:00	Inclusion	DG			
4	8:15	Morning Work	CJ, AN, DG, YE			
5	8:30	Morning Meeting	CJ, AN, DG, YE			
6	8:45	Phonics	CJ, AN, DG, YE			
7	9:00	Read Aloud	CJ, AN, DG, YE			
8	9:15	ELA Center 1	CJ, AN, DG, YE		██████	
9	9:30	ELA Center 2	CJ, AN, DG, YE		██████	
10	9:45	ELA Center 3	CJ, AN, DG, YE		██████	
11	10:00	ELA Center 4	CJ, AN, DG, YE		██████	
12	10:15	Pre-vocational	CJ, AN			
13	10:30	Pre-vocational	CJ, AN			

The next step is to take your schedule, as the teacher, and fill in what you are doing throughout the day. For example, under morning work I may put that I am completing attendance and checking student folders for parent communication. For reading aloud, I would put that

I am leading the read aloud activity. I do not put specific students' names down as my focus is on teaching the activity.

You can also write, see lesson plans for more details, when there is a substitute. An instructional matrix is wonderful to have in your substitute binder.

When I get to an activity, such as centers, I will put the specific student's name in my column. I try to keep the center rotations the same for at least the quarter to help my students learn their schedules. The consistency of their center rotation schedule also helps them to become more independent during their transitions in the classroom.

	A	B	C	D	E	F	G
1	TIME	Activity	Student(s)	Ms. Crews	Para 1 - Lauren	1-on-1 - Ashley	
2	7:45	Arrival	CJ, AN, DG, YE	Bus Duty			
3	8:00	Inclusion	CJ, AN	CJ, AN			
4	8:15	Morning Work	CJ, AN, DG, YE	Check student folders, complete attendance, return any paperwork			
5	8:30	Morning Meeting	CJ, AN, DG, YE	Lead morning meeting - see lesson plans for more details			
6	8:45	Phonics	CJ, AN, DG, YE	Lead phonics activities - see lesson plans for more details			
7	9:00	Read Aloud	CJ, AN, DG, YE	Lead read aloud activities - see lesson plans for more details			
8	9:15	ELA Center 1	CJ, AN, DG, YE	Intervention lessons and IEP goal work - DG			
9	9:30	ELA Center 2	CJ, AN, DG, YE	Intervention lessons and IEP goal work - CJ			

Once you have completed your schedule, you need to add in the schedules of any other adults in your room. For my classroom, I assign the students to each adult for each 15-minute time block. The purpose of this is to make sure if there are any behavioral needs, all adults know who handles the situation is using the appropriate behavioral response from the behavior system. (See section 2 for more information on behavior systems)

Some adults will have multiple students assigned to them at one time. I base who is assigned together by their behavioral and academic needs. When you are writing out what each adult is to be doing, include any specific accommodations that need to be utilized. For example, during morning work, you might have, "Support Sabrina and Hannah to complete their work using the prompt hierarchy. Support Sabrina by reading aloud any text." You want to continue like this for all the adults for the entire day.

	A	B	C	D	E	F	G
1	TIME	Activity	Student(s)	Ms. Crews	Para 1 - Lauren	1-on-1 - Ashley	
2	7:45	Arrival	CJ, AN, DG, YE	Bus Duty	Car duty AN, DG	Bus Duty YE, CJ	
3	8:00	Inclusion	CJ, AN	CJ, AN	DG	YE	
4	8:15	Morning Work	CJ, AN, DG, YE	Check student folders, complete attendance, return any paperwork	AN, DG - support morning work activities using the prompt hierarchy	YE, CJ - support morning work activities using the prompt hierarchy	
5	8:30	Morning Meeting	CJ, AN, DG, YE	Lead morning meeting - see lesson plans for more details	AN, DG - support participation in morning meeting using the prompt hierarchy	YE, CJ - support participation in morning meeting using the prompt hierarchy	
6	8:45	Phonics	CJ, AN, DG, YE	Lead phonics activities - see lesson plans for more details	AN, DG - support participation in phonics activities using the prompt hierarchy	YE, CJ - support participation in phonics activities using the prompt hierarchy	
7	9:00	Read Aloud	CJ, AN, DG, YE	Lead read aloud activities - see lesson plans for more details	AN, DG - support participation in read aloud using the prompt hierarchy	YE, CJ - support participation in read aloud using the prompt hierarchy	
8	9:15	ELA Center 1	CJ, AN, DG, YE	Intervention lessons and IEP goal work - DG	DTT - use student binders to determine what curriculum to work on with the students	YE - support during center activities using the prompt hierarchy	

At this point, the matrix itself will be completed, but there is still another step. You want to make a note of anything you need to provide training. This should also include training on reading and using the matrix. I recommend training all of your paraprofessionals on everything in the matrix in the case of an absence without a substitute you can have your other adults fill in as needed.

After you have finished training the adults, you want to post your matrix in your classroom so everyone can access it. I also recommend putting it in your substitute binder.

SYSTEMS FOR TRAINING PARAPROFESSIONALS
With your completed instructional matrix, you should have a list of topics for training at the beginning of the year. This is what I recommend starting with. You will then need to make a system for how

you will continue training your paraprofessionals throughout the school year.

The goal for this system can be to create a method for continual education of the paraprofessionals in your classroom. This system will depend on your district guidelines regarding meetings and work hours. Because of this, I recommend making a system that will work for training face to face or using handouts/videos.

You will need to determine how often you will meet, how you will meet, and what you will discuss. I recommend keeping each meeting, face to face or handout/videos, to one topic.

When you are training, I recommend you follow a teach, implement, reflect protocol in your system. For this protocol, you will teach the topic to your paraprofessionals. For the period of time between the next meeting, they will implement the topic. Finally, when you come back together for your next meeting, you will have your paraprofessionals reflect on implementing the topic.

For example, you plan to meet face to face on a monthly basis. For your first topic, you train your paraprofessionals on how to implement discrete trial training. Then, for the next month, you have your paraprofessionals implement discrete trial training with your students. Finally, when you meet again next month, have your paraprofessionals complete a reflection and provide feedback on how discrete trial training is implemented in your classroom.

When deciding what topics to train your paraprofessionals, I recommend starting with the list you made while creating your activity matrix. I believe you should provide direct training on your expectations for the paraprofessionals in your classroom. You can ask the paraprofessionals on which topics they would like more training. And finally, pay attention to the needs of your classroom as the need for training arises.

SECTION 5: SYSTEMS FOR PAPERWORK

Paperwork is a hallmark of special education. If we aren't teaching, we are working on paperwork. There are two big areas of paperwork I think of: data collection and IEPs.

SYSTEMS FOR DATA COLLECTION

With every student having at least one IEP goal and needing to write reports of progress, data collection systems are extremely important. In my district, we have to take data on each goal at a minimum of once every two weeks. Ideally, they would have us take data on each goal once a week. This can prove challenging if you do not have a system set up for taking data.

There are a few questions you need to ask yourself as you are planning your data collection system:

- How often will you take data?
- Who will take data?
- Will you use a paper system or an electronic system?

I recommend taking data at least once every other week. Personally, I aim for once a week for each goal. You can have your paraprofessionals help with data collection, so it is easier to gather data once a week.

If you choose to use a paper system, there are a variety of options you can use.

For data sheets you can have one goal per sheet and use the same sheet the entire year, such as a trial-by-trial data sheet. You can have a sheet that has all the goals for one student that you use each week. Another option is to group goals by subject and use a new sheet each week. This option is useful for taking data during small group time.

Sabrina's Goals
Date:

Given a field of 2 and the prompt "touch___", Sabrina will receptively identify the uppercase letters of her first name with 80% accuracy on 4 out of 5 data opportunities.

Trial	S	A	B	R	I	N
1						
2						
3						
4						
5						
Accuracy						

Given a familiar story read to her, Sabrina will retell 3 things (character, setting, events, etc.) from the story with 80% accuracy across 3 consecutive data days.

1	2	3	Accuracy

Sabrina

Given a field of 2 and the prompt "touch___", Sabrina will receptively identify the uppercase letters of her first name with 80% accuracy on 4 out of 5 data opportunities.	5 4 3 2 1 0 ND	5 4 3 2 1 0 ND	5 4 3 2 1 0 ND	5 4 3 2 1 0 ND	5 4 3 2 1 0 ND	5 4 3 2 1 0 ND	5 4 3 2 1 0 ND	5 4 3 2 1 0 ND	5 4 3 2 1 0 ND	5 4 3 2 1 0 ND	5 4 3 2 1 0 ND	5 4 3 2 1 0 ND	5 4 3 2 1 0 ND	5 4 3 2 1 0 ND	5 4 3 2 1 0 ND	5 4 3 2 1 0 ND	5 4 3 2 1 0 ND	5 4 3 2 1 0 ND	5 4 3 2 1 0 ND	5 4 3 2 1 0 ND
Accuracy:																				
Given a familiar story read to her, Sabrina will retell 3 things (character, setting, events, etc.) from the story with 80% accuracy across 3 consecutive data days.	5 4 3 2 1 0 ND	5 4 3 2 1 0 ND	5 4 3 2 1 0 ND	5 4 3 2 1 0 ND	5 4 3 2 1 0 ND	5 4 3 2 1 0 ND	5 4 3 2 1 0 ND	5 4 3 2 1 0 ND	5 4 3 2 1 0 ND	5 4 3 2 1 0 ND	5 4 3 2 1 0 ND	5 4 3 2 1 0 ND	5 4 3 2 1 0 ND	5 4 3 2 1 0 ND	5 4 3 2 1 0 ND	5 4 3 2 1 0 ND	5 4 3 2 1 0 ND	5 4 3 2 1 0 ND	5 4 3 2 1 0 ND	5 4 3 2 1 0 ND
Accuracy:																				
Given a familiar story read to her, Sabrina will retell 3 things (character, setting, events, etc.) from the story with 80% accuracy across 3 consecutive data days.	5 4 3 2 1 0 ND	5 4 3 2 1 0 ND	5 4 3 2 1 0 ND	5 4 3 2 1 0 ND	5 4 3 2 1 0 ND	5 4 3 2 1 0 ND	5 4 3 2 1 0 ND	5 4 3 2 1 0 ND	5 4 3 2 1 0 ND	5 4 3 2 1 0 ND	5 4 3 2 1 0 ND	5 4 3 2 1 0 ND	5 4 3 2 1 0 ND	5 4 3 2 1 0 ND	5 4 3 2 1 0 ND	5 4 3 2 1 0 ND	5 4 3 2 1 0 ND	5 4 3 2 1 0 ND	5 4 3 2 1 0 ND	5 4 3 2 1 0 ND
Accuracy:																				

5 – Independent within the classroom
4 – Verbal prompt
3 – Visual prompt (model, point, picture)
2 – Partial physical prompt
1 – Physical prompt
0 – Child does not respond/tantrums
ND – No data for the session

Sabrina

Given a field of 2 and the prompt "touch___", Sabrina will receptively identify the uppercase letters of her first name with 80% accuracy on 4 out of 5 data opportunities.

Instructor														
1														
2														
3														
4														
5														
6														
7														
8														
9														
10														

Graph

100														
90														
80														
70														
60														
50														
40														
30														
20														
10														
0														

Once you have figured out which data sheet you will use, I recommend color coding the sheets so you can quickly grab the sheets you need for the student you are working with. You can also store them on clipboards with a color-coded top sheet.

Data cards can have the same setup as data sheets just in a smaller size, such as an index card. The most common data cards are ones that have one goal and space to take data for the entire year. There are data cards that have one goal with only one data point, however I find this is difficult to manage as you have a lot of cards throughout the entire year. Data cards are best for a single student per card as the size makes it difficult for multiple students.

Sabrina   Date:

Given a field of 2 and the prompt "touch____", Sabrina will receptively identify the uppercase letters of her first name with 80% accuracy on 4 out of 5 data opportunities.

S	A	B	R	I	N

Sabrina

Given a field of 2 and the prompt "touch____", Sabrina will receptively identify the uppercase letters of her first name with 80% accuracy on 4 out of 5 data opportunities.

A	S	O	N	D	J	F	M	A	M

Once you have set up your data cards, you can put them on a binder ring. I recommend color coding the data cards so you can quickly grab the correct set of cards for the student you are working with.

If you have chosen a paper system but must input the data into a digital database, such as Ed Plan, you will need to include when you will input the data in your system. I like to take time during my planning on Friday to input the information. Doing it consistently makes it easier when writing reports of progress. You can however batch input the data when you are writing your report of progress.

For electronic systems you can set up a form in something like Google©
Forms. Here, you can set up drop-down menus for students and goals
with a place to put the data as well. This way you can use one form for
all of your students and all of their goals. If you have a program, such as
Ed Plan, you can also just input the data directly as you work with the
students.

If you choose to you an electronic system, you want to make sure you
and whoever is helping you take data, has consistent access to
technology. What is great about Google© Forms is that the form can be
filled out by phone.

Once you have decided how often you will take data, who will take the
data, and how you will take the data, you want to train anyone who will
use this system. Because we take data from the beginning of the year, I
recommend that you train anyone on your data collection system prior
to the start of the year.

Systems for IEPs

It is hard to think of systems in special education without thinking about
IEPs. So much of our time goes into IEPs. While I will not be discussing
how to write an IEP, I will go into how to organize the process.

The first thing you need to do is make a list of the due dates of everyone
on your caseload. List them in order from the first month of the school
year until the last. You also want to make a note of any evaluations that
may be due during this year. On this list, I also like to note any related
services the student receives and parent contact information.

The next step is to get a manila folder and label it with the student's
name and IEP due date. In this folder you are going to place any blank
present level assessment sheets and checklists. Any forms that general
education teachers or parents would need to fill out for input should
also be placed in the folder. Place a copy of the parents' rights booklet
in the student's home language. I use a generic meeting agenda for
annual meetings, and I also place a copy of the agenda in the folder.
Once all of the of the folders are created, file them in due date order.

In my district, IEP meetings are scheduled eight weeks out from the due date. At the beginning of each month, I go in and pull the folders of every student who is due in the next two months. Because everything I need is already in the folder, I can move to taking present level data.

If they have taken any online assessments, such as the iReady© diagnostic, I will print out those results and put them in the folder. I will also give any checklists or data forms to the general education teachers to provide input on the IEP. If you send any paperwork home for parent input prior to the meeting, I will send those home as well. As forms are returned to you, place them in the folder.

Once you have given all of your present level assessments and received any forms for the parents and general education teachers, you can sit down and write the IEP. Everything you need to write the IEP will be in the folder.

In the state of Tennessee, it is a law that a draft IEP must be provided to the parents 48 hours prior to the meeting. Please check with your state and district regarding writing a draft IEP. Whether you write a draft before the meeting or write the IEP in the meeting, everything you need will be complied in the student folder.

The way you run your meeting may differ depending on the requirements of your district. However, I recommend using as much parent-friendly language as possible.

After the meeting, you want to place the signed documents in the student folder until you can file them in the student's cumulative record. Once all of the documents have been filed, you want to update the student folder with the new IEP due date and refill with the blank documents.

I highly recommend putting a checklist of these steps on the front of the student folder to check off as you go through this process. I have found that if you have an organized system for the IEP process, you are less likely to miss steps or lose paperwork.

Student Name:
IEP Due Date:
Eligibility Due Date:

Prior to meeting and creation of draft
- Present Level Data
- Contact parents to set a date
- Create and send home an invite
  - Document on contacts page
- Create an outlook invitation on SPED Calendar

Draft
- Narratives
  - Strength
  - Parent concerns are left blank
  - Adverse impact of disability
- Present Levels of performance
- Goals
- Accommodations
  - Classroom
  - State testing
  - District testing
- Services – LEAVE BLANK
- Send home 48 hours prior to meeting
  - Document on contacts page

Meeting
- Project IEP Draft and make edits in real time
- Finalize, print, and send home at meeting
- Write prior written notice in meeting
- Fax
- File

After
- Provide updated IEP at a glance

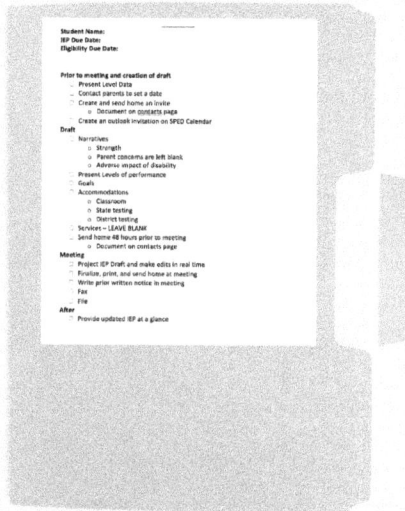

Implementing systems in your classroom will save time, provide accountability, consistency, and efficiency. Building systems in your classroom will take time. Start with one system. Learn about that system, plan it out, implement it, and reflect. Once that system is implementing and running efficiently, add on another system. Follow this same process until you have systemized your classroom.

www.ingramcontent.com/pod-product-compliance
Lightning Source LLC
Chambersburg PA
CBHW061042110426
42740CB00050B/2871